c.1

DATE DUE

JUN 19 '04			
FE 15 '05			

WORLD ALMANAC® LIBRARY OF THE STATES

Washington

THE EVERGREEN STATE

by Rachel Barenblat

Curriculum Consultant: Jean Craven,
Director of Instructional Support,
Albuquerque, NM, Public Schools

WORLD ALMANAC® LIBRARY

Please visit our web site at: www.worldalmanaclibrary.com
For a free color catalog describing World Almanac® Library's list of high-quality books
and multimedia programs, call 1-800-848-2928 or fax your request to (414) 332-3567.

Library of Congress Cataloging-in-Publication Data

Barenblat, Rachel.
    Washington, the Evergreen State / by Rachel Barenblat.
       p. cm. — (World Almanac Library of the states)
    Includes bibliographical references and index.
    Summary: Illustrations and text present the history, geography, people, politics and
government, economy, and social life and customs of the state of Washington.
    ISBN 0-8368-5122-6 (lib. bdg.)
    ISBN 0-8368-5294-X (softcover)
    1. Washington (State)—Juvenile literature. [1. Washington (State).] I. Title. II. Series.
F891.3.B47   2002
979.7—dc21   2001046992

This edition first published in 2002 by
World Almanac® Library
330 West Olive Street, Suite 100
Milwaukee, WI 53212 USA

This edition © 2002 by World Almanac® Library.

Design and Editorial: **Jack&Bill**/Bill SMITH STUDIO Inc.
Editors: Jackie Ball and Kristen Behrens
Art Directors: Ron Leighton and Jeffrey Rutzky
Photo Research and Buying: Christie Silver and Sean Livingstone
Design and Production: Maureen O'Connor and Jeffrey Rutzky
World Almanac® Library Editors: Patricia Lantier, Amy Stone, Valerie J. Weber,
Catherine Gardner, Carolyn Kott Washburne, Alan Wachtel, Monica Rausch
World Almanac® Library Production: Scott M. Krall, Eva Erato-Rudek, Tammy Gruenewald

Photo credits: p. 4 courtesy of Experience Music Project; p. 6 (clockwise) © Corel, © PhotoDisc,
© Corel; p. 7 (top) © Corel, (bottom) © Bettmann/CORBIS; p. 9 © PhotoDisc; p. 10 © Corel;
p. 11 © Library of Congress; p. 12 © Corel; p. 13 © Library of Congress; pp. 14–17 courtesy of
MSCUA, University of Washington; p. 18 © Nick Gunderson; p. 19 © S. Vento; p. 20–21 © Corel;
p. 23 © Painet; p. 26 (from left to right) © PhotoDisc, courtesy of Boeing; p. 27 courtesy of
Microsoft Corporation; p. 29 © S. Vento; p. 30 courtesy of Washington State House of
Representatives; p. 31 © Anthony Bolante/TimePix; p. 33 (top) © Painet, (bottom) © Charles J.
Peterson/TimePix; p. 34 © Experience Music Project; p. 35 © Library of Congress; p. 36
courtesy of Washington State Parks and Recreation Commission; p. 37 © Reuters/TimePix;
p. 38 © ArtToday; p. 39 © PhotoDisc; p. 40 © Hulton-Deutsch/Corbis; p. 41 © Reuters/TimePix;
pp. 42–43 © Library of Congress; p. 42 © PhotoDisc; p. 43 (top) © PhotoDisc, (bottom) © Corel

Printed in the United States of America

1 2 3 4 5 6 7 8 9 06 05 04 03 02

Washington

Ready to Rumble

Washington is a place of astounding beauty and astounding contrasts. Separated by the high Cascade Mountains, the state's eastern and western regions possess climates and terrains that are completely different. In the east the state can be so dry some of it looks like desert. Meanwhile the west is legendarily wet. Although the reputation is somewhat unjustly earned, Seattle is famous for being one long, rainy day. In the east stretch apple orchards and endless fields of wheat. In the west temperate rain forests are home to birds and wildlife. The west is also full of the hemlocks, firs, and pines that have earned Washington its nickname — the Evergreen State.

Beneath all that natural beauty, however, is natural danger. The Cascades were created by violent shifts in Earth's crust, and the movement is still going on. Washington is part of the Ring of Fire, the region where moving tectonic plates meet in the lands encircling the Pacific Ocean. In 1980 Mount St. Helens erupted violently. Mount Rainier — so close to Seattle you can see it from downtown — is an active volcano. Experts are watching it carefully, so they can be ready for an eruption.

Washingtonians have a tradition of unrest, especially when it comes to injustice. They have never been shy about speaking out — sometimes forcefully. Back in 1854 Chief Sealth (Seattle) of the Salish people argued that land could not be owned by individuals. That spirit has led to a tradition of environmentalism and some of the toughest environmental laws in the country.

In 1909 workers challenged laws prohibiting free speech in their attempt to organize labor, and won. More than ninety years later, protesters turned downtown Seattle into a combat zone as they demonstrated against the World Trade Organization (WTO). Freethinkers as diverse as Bill Gates and Jimi Hendrix have found Washington a welcome home. People in love with the land and with an active intellectual and spiritual life will continue to flock to this verdant Pacific state.

▶ Map of Washington showing interstate highway system, as well as major cities and waterways.

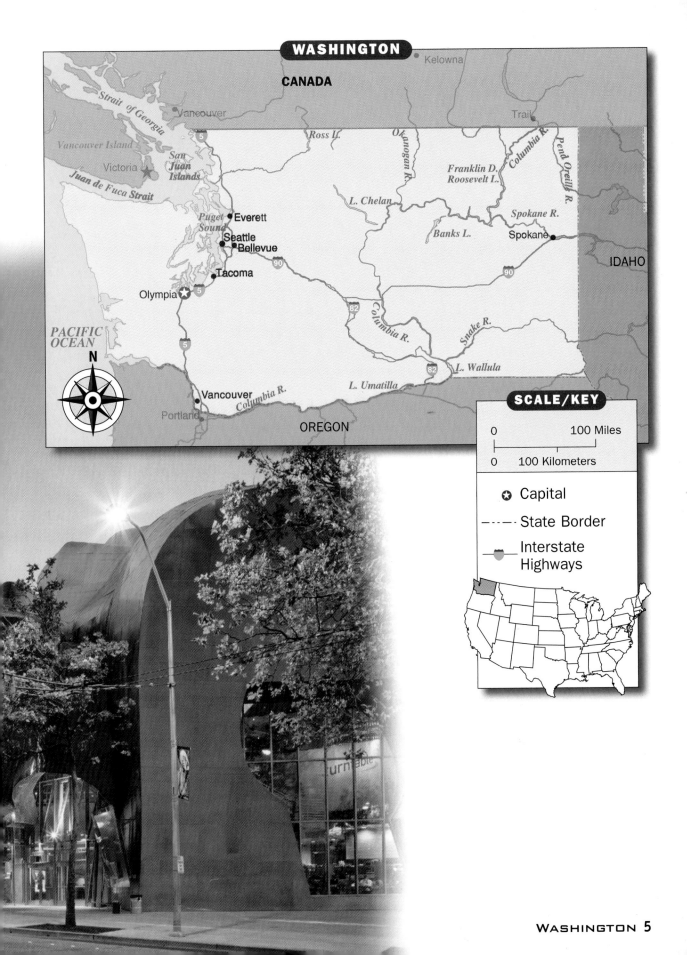

CANADA

Kelowna

Trail

Strait of Georgia

Vancouver

Ross L.

Okanogan R.

Columbia R.

Pend Oreille R.

Vancouver Island

Victoria

San Juan Islands

Franklin D. Roosevelt L.

Juan de Fuca Strait

L. Chelan

Spokane R.

Puget Sound

Everett

Banks L.

Spokane

Seattle

Bellevue

IDAHO

Tacoma

Olympia

Columbia R.

PACIFIC OCEAN

N

Snake R.

L. Wallula

Vancouver

Columbia R.

L. Umatilla

Portland

OREGON

SCALE/KEY

| 0 | 100 Miles |

| 0 | 100 Kilometers |

⊗ Capital

--·-- State Border

Interstate Highways

Fast Facts

Washington (WA), The Evergreen State

Entered Union

November 11, 1889 (42nd state)

Capital	Population
Olympia	42,514

Total Population (2000)

5,894,121 (15th most populous state)

Largest Cities	Population
Seattle	563,374
Spokane	195,629
Tacoma	193,556
Vancouver	143,560
Bellevue	109,569

Land Area

66,544 square miles (172,349 square kilometers) (20th largest state)

State Motto

"Al-ki" or "Alki" — *a Native American word meaning "by and by."*

State Song

"Washington, My Home" *by Helen Davis and Stuart Churchill*

State Bird

Willow Goldfinch or Wild Canary

State Fish

Steelhead Trout — *The steelhead trout is an anadromous fish, a fish that returns to freshwater to spawn. It is also one of the most popular catches for recreational fishing, which is very popular in Washington.*

State Insect

Green Darner Dragonfly — *Also known as the "mosquito hawk," this dragonfly is a beneficial contributor to the state's ecosystem because it consumes a large number of insect pests.*

State Tree

Western Hemlock

State Flower

Coast Rhododendron

State Fruit

Apple — *The apple was named a state symbol in 1989, Washington's centennial year. The apple comes in many different colors, sizes, and varieties. Washington is the nation's top apple-producing state.*

State Gem

Petrified Wood — *The best place in the state to see petrified wood is the Gingko Petrified Forest State Park in Vantage. Petrified wood looks like the wood it came from, but it's really rock.*

State Fossil

Columbian Mammoth — *Fossils of the Columbian mammoth, Washington's newest state symbol, were found on Washington's Olympic Peninsula.*

PLACES TO VISIT

San Juan Islands Many islands and islets make up the San Juan Islands. Eagles nest here and pods of orcas ("killer whales") feed in the rich waters. Visitors can stay on the islands of Lopez, Shaw, Orcas, and San Juan and enjoy hiking, biking, and wildlife viewing.

Space Needle, *Seattle*
Edward E. Carlson penciled his vision of the Space Needle on a place mat in a coffeehouse. That futuristic image would become the towering centerpiece of the 1962 Seattle World's Fair and an internationally recognized symbol of the city. The observation deck and revolving restaurant allow visitors to gaze out over the city from above 500 feet (152 meters).

For other places and events, see p. 44. For other places and events, see p. 44.

BIGGEST, BEST, AND MOST

- Hell's Canyon, near Clarkston, is the deepest river canyon in the United States. It is almost 8,000 feet (2,438 m) from the top of the cliff to the bottom of the river.

- The Grand Coulee Dam is the largest concrete structure in the United States. The dam's twenty-four generators produce 6.5 million kilowatts of electricity, making it the largest single source of power in the Northwest.

- The Boeing Commercial Airplane Factory, in Everett, is the largest building in the world. Workers use bicycles to get around inside.

- Washington is number one in the nation in the production of apples; lentils; dry, edible peas; hops; pears; red raspberries; spearmint oil; and sweet cherries.

STATE FIRSTS

In 1996 Gary Locke became Washington's twenty-first governor and the first Chinese-American state governor in U.S. history.

Big Blast

Mount St. Helens erupted on May 18, 1980, with an explosion five hundred times greater than the atomic bomb dropped on Hiroshima, Japan. The boom could be heard all the way to Canada. Ash and rock blew out of the side of the mountain at 450 miles (724 km) per hour, and a thick layer of ash blanketed a wide area. Fifty-seven people were killed. Millions of trees were blasted into toothpicks. Twenty years after this volcano's amazing eruption, though, visitors can see the land being reborn as plants sprout through the surreal moonscape of rocks and ash.

Bigfoot

Though the creature also known as Sasquatch (from the Native American Salish language *se'sxac,* meaning "wild men") probably doesn't exist, it can be fun to imagine that it does. There have been numerous — but unconfirmed — sightings around Washington State and the northwestern part of the country. Sasquatch is usually described as a primate (the same order as humans, but also including apes) ranging from 6 to 15 feet (2–4.5 m) tall, standing on two feet, and giving off a foul smell. Footprints have measured up to 24 inches (60 centimeters) in length and 8 inches (20 cm) in width — a big foot indeed!

Northwest Passage

> This plain stretched to the foot of a connected body of mountains, which, excepting between the west and north-west, were not very remote; and even in that quarter the country might be considered as moderately elevated, bounded by distant stupendous mountains covered with snow, and apparently detached from each other; though possibly they might be connected by land of insufficient height to intercept our horizon.
>
> — *George Vancouver,* Voyage of Discovery to the North Pacific Ocean, and Round the World, *1798*

Early History

Most historians and anthroplogists believe that the earliest inhabitants of the west coast of North America probably arrived twenty thousand years ago. Four tribal groups settled what is now called Washington. They developed distinctive cultures because the landscape and the climate varied so greatly between the western coastal part of the state and the eastern plateau region.

Coastal Peoples

The Chinook lived along the lower Columbia River and the coast. They spoke a group of languages called Chinookan. The Chinook were famous traders, with connections stretching as far as the Great Plains. The river was a rich source of salmon, the basis of the area's economy, and many groups traded with the Chinook for dried fish. The first Europeans to meet the Chinook were the explorers Meriwether Lewis and William Clark, who encountered them in 1805.

The Coast Salish lived in most of western Washington state, especially in the Puget Sound area. Like the Chinook and other peoples of the Pacific Northwest coast, they lived primarily on fish. Also like the Chinook, the Coast Salish celebrated community with elaborate *potlatch* ceremonies in which gifts were distributed among the tribe.

Native Americans of Washington

Cayuse
Chinook
Clallam
Coast Salish
Colville
Kalispel
Klickitat
Lummi
Makah
Mojave
Nez Percé
Nisqually
Nooksak
Okanigan
Puyallup
Quinault
Salish
Snohomish
Spokane
Walla Walla
Yakima

Plateau Peoples

The Nez Percé spoke Sahaptian and were called various names by various people. The name we know them by, Nez Percé, is French for "pierced nose," and refers to their nose pendants. Because they lived in the eastern part of the state, the Nez Percé were influenced by the Plains Indians living just east of the Rocky Mountains. They lived in small villages located on salmon streams, hunted game, and gathered plants. Their dwellings were communal lodges, which sometimes held as many as thirty families. Like the Nez Percé, the Yakima spoke Sahaptian. They lived in south-central Washington and were primarily salmon fishers.

▼ Mt. Rainier is both an active volcano and the largest mountain in Washington State. It is 14,410 feet (4,392 m) tall — the largest mountain in the Cascade Range. The oldest known archeological sites on the mountain date back 2,300 to 4,500 years ago.

The Earliest Explorers

Washington's earliest explorers came from many lands, including Spain, England, and Greece. Most of them were searching for the fabled Northwest Passage, a hoped-for waterway connecting the Atlantic and Pacific Oceans.

A Greek explorer named Apostolos Valerianos is believed to have entered the strait between Washington and Canada's Vancouver Island in 1592. He was known by the name Juan de Fuca. When the American explorer Charles Barkely sailed there in 1787, he named the strait after de Fuca. In the late 1700s several Spanish explorers sailed up from Mexico into the Olympic Peninsula region. In 1775 Bruno Heceta and Juan de Bodega y Quadra claimed the land for Spain.

In 1778 the British explorer Captain James Cook sailed along the coast of what is now Washington and acquired a wealth of otter furs from Native Americans. This marked the start of the fur trade. In 1792 Great Britain sent an explorer named George Vancouver to find the Northwest Passage and map the coast. At the same time Robert Gray was exploring Washington for the United States. Gray sailed from Boston to the Pacific Northwest on a trading expedition in 1787 and traveled around the world, reaching Boston again in August 1790. In May 1792, while on a

◄ Olympia National Forest is one of Washington's untouched wilderness areas and one of the world's few temperate rain forests. Rain forests receive as much as 124 inches (315 cm) of rain annually. This forest is also home to a one-thousand-year-old spruce, the world's largest. It stands 191 feet (58 m) tall and measures 59 feet (18 m) in circumference.

second voyage in his ship *Columbia,* Gray explored what is now Grays Harbor and the Columbia River.

In 1803 President Thomas Jefferson sent Lewis and Clark to explore the land that the United States had just bought from France in the Louisiana Purchase. In the Rocky Mountains the two explorers crossed the Continental Divide (the place that defines the way rivers flow: east of the Divide, rivers flow into the Atlantic; west of the Divide, they flow into the Pacific) and canoed along several rivers until they reached the Columbia River and the Pacific Ocean in 1805. They reported back, telling of the amazing country they had seen. As a result, several fur-trading companies established outposts in Washington.

Mission Accomplished

After fur traders, the earliest immigrants into Washington were missionaries. Marcus Whitman and Henry Spalding were among the first missionaries to take the Oregon Trail in 1836. Whitman and Spalding brought the first white women — their wives Narcissa Whitman and Eliza Spalding — and the first wheeled vehicle — the cart in which Narcissa rode — into Washington. In 1847 measles broke out among the Cayuse of Whitman's mission. The disease spread, rapidly killing fourteen of the Cayuse. Blaming the Whitmans, a group of Cayuse killed them and sixteen other white settlers in the mission.

Other missionaries followed, however, and their presence encouraged further white settlement. Once the trail became familiar, more people moved to the region.

Territory and State

In a rush for new land, both Britain and the United States claimed the region, which was then called Oregon Country and included parts of what are now several states and British Columbia. After the War of 1812, the Treaty of

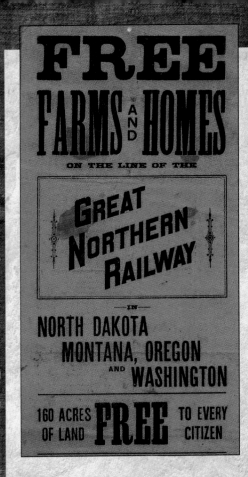

Dawes General Allotment Act

Relations with Native tribes suffered a major blow in 1887 with the Dawes General Allotment Act, which forced individual Native Americans to choose their own 160-acre (65-ha) plots. White settlers were also allowed to choose land on what had been Indian reservations. Private ownership of land went against Native American tradition. Earlier, in 1854, Chief Sealth of the Salish people asked:

> *How can you buy or sell the sky, the warmth of the land? The idea is strange to us. If we do not own the freshness of the air and the sparkle of the water, how can you buy them?*

The city of Seattle is named after the white settlers' pronunciation of Sealth's name.

Ghent gave both countries the right to the region for a period of ten years. That agreement was renewed twice before the land was divided in 1846.

Washington Territory was established in 1853, and its first governor was Isaac Stevens, an engineer and soldier. His main task was to gain control of Native American lands. To this end he signed treaties with many tribal groups. Most Native Americans were initially receptive to European and American settlers, whether fur traders or missionaries. However, not all settlers were friendly — and many of the treaties Governor Stevens implemented were very unfair. This led to several major conflicts between the Native Americans and the white settlers, who had the full support of the U.S. Army. In 1855 a number of Native American nations united under Yakima's Chief Kamaiakan, who declared his intention to drive all whites from the region. Three years of raids and ambushes followed, until September 1858, when the Native Americans were defeated at the Battle of Four Lakes (on a tributary of the Spokane River).

An 1855 treaty between the Nez Percé and the United States created a large Nez Percé reservation, encompassing most of their traditional land. When gold was discovered on

▼ A reenactment of the pioneer journey through Washington on the Oregon Trail.

the Salmon and Clearwater Rivers in 1860, U.S. commissioners decided to rewrite the treaty and reduced the size of the reservation by three-fourths. Many Nez Percé never accepted either the old treaty or the new, and hostile actions and raids by both whites and Native Americans evolved into the Nez Percé War of 1877.

For five months a small band of 250 Nez Percé warriors, under the leadership of Chief Joseph, held off a U.S. force of five thousand troops led by General O. O. Howard, who tracked the Nez Percé through Idaho, Wyoming, and Montana before they surrendered to General Nelson A. Miles on October 5. The Nez Percé were sent to an area in Oklahoma that was rife with malaria rather than back to the Northwest as promised.

The (Rail)Road to Statehood

In 1869 the first U.S. transcontinental railroad opened. It went to California, however, and the Northwest remained isolated. In 1883 the Northern Pacific Railroad Company's tracks finally met those of the Oregon Railway and Navigation Company, creating a new northern route. Thousands of settlers poured into the state, as the combination of railroad and telegraph strengthened Washington Territory's ties with the United States.

Settlers flooded into the region, ranching sheep, farming wheat and produce, and creating many small cities, including Spokane. The population of Washington grew fivefold from 1881 to 1890, reaching almost 360,000. By 1920 it reached almost 1,360,000. In 1889 the territory became a state. Washington's first state governor, Elisha Ferry, took the oath of office one week after statehood was declared.

The Twentieth Century

In 1909 the people of the Pacific Northwest were hopeful for their future. They held a great fair — the Alaska-Yukon-Pacific Exposition — celebrating the region. However, not everything in the Pacific Northwest was easy. Because the timber industry and the railroads employed so many workers in Washington, the state became an important center for the labor union movement. At the turn of the century, many

The Great Fire

You wouldn't know it from walking the sidewalks of Seattle's historic Pioneer Square, but underneath lies a whole other Seattle. When the Great Fire of Seattle destroyed most of the city in 1889, the opportunity was seized for a new beginning. Originally, the city was built on coastal mudflats, which made it legendarily dirty and difficult to get around. After the fire, a new city was built 15 feet (4.5 m) above the old city. Remnants of the old city were left underground, but today they can be visited in one of Seattle's most unusual tourist attractions, an underground walking tour.

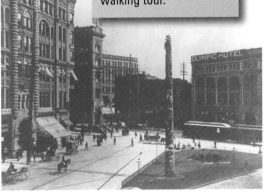

▲ Pioneer Square in Seattle, circa 1906, rebuilt after the Great Fire.

Chinese people came to Washington. Competition for jobs created racial tensions, and there were riots against the Chinese in some mining camps and fruit orchards. The International Workers of the World (I.W.W.), known as Wobblies, decided that the problem was not with their fellow workers — whatever their race — but with the employers and the overall economic system. They were successful for a time in gaining more rights for workers but lost public support when they opposed the nation's entry into World War I.

World War II

America's involvement in World War II began on December 7, 1941, when Japan bombed Pearl Harbor in Hawaii. Many Washingtonians feared that their state, too, would be vulnerable to Japanese bombers. The people who lived around Puget Sound were ordered to hang blackout curtains in their windows at night so no light would be visible and bombers would have more difficulty finding their targets.

Washington grew rapidly after World War II. The population skyrocketed, but growth occurred with few planning or zoning laws. When the region's natural beauty

The World's Fair

In the mid-1950s a group of executives met to plan an anniversary celebration of the Alaska-Yukon-Pacific Exposition, which had taken place in Seattle in 1909. Their plan turned into the World's Fair of 1962. They rebuilt downtown Seattle for the occasion, creating the Space Needle as a futuristic theme for the fair. That year millions of tourists visited Seattle.

started to suffer — Lake Washington, for instance, became very polluted — new councils were formed to clean up the environment.

Civil Rights

The 1900s brought more struggles between the races. African Americans had long had a presence in Washington's major cities, but many more came early in the twentieth century. Thousands of Latinos also came during World War II to replace absent field-workers. Asians continued to arrive in large numbers. These groups were not always welcomed. The civil rights movement brought difficult changes to Washington, and in the 1960s some protests in Seattle and Tacoma turned violent.

Another struggle took place in the latter part of the twentieth century between Native Americans and environmentalists. In the 1850s territorial governor Isaac Stevens signed treaties allowing Native people to keep their right to fish in the region. By the turn of the century, however, commercial fishing had depleted fishing stocks. Environmentalists fought to preserve the fish, bringing them into conflict with fishers, including Native Americans. In 1974 a federal judge decided the original treaties were valid and Native Americans therefore had the right to fish wherever and however they had traditionally fished. Native Americans and environmentalists are now trying to work together to cope with the shrinking fish supply.

New Economy?

Washington state has led two of the twentieth century's greatest industrial revolutions. It was long the headquarters of Boeing, the world's biggest aircraft manufacturer, and is still the location for many of the company's factories. Lately the state has become even better known as the location of Microsoft, a computer software company founded by Bill Gates and Paul Allen in the late 1970s. Many other computer companies have since started up in the region. Washingtonians hope the wave of Internet commerce can provide jobs and a stable economy without the negative environmental side effects of heavy industry. It remains to be seen whether this New Economy can live up to its promise.

"Wobbly" Workers

Spokane in 1909 was the center of a rich mining, lumber, and farm area. Many migrant workers toiled long hours in unsafe conditions for low wages. The International Workers of the World, known as Wobblies, tried to unionize these workers. Spokane authorities refused to allow the Wobblies to speak publicly. When one speaker was jailed, another stepped up. Nearly twelve hundred people were jailed before the mayor allowed their right to free speech. This landmark in U.S. labor history became known as the Spokane Free Speech Fight.

The Immediate Demands of the I. W. W.

The Spirit of the Times

Rich, Healthy, Carefree...

Enthusiastically Western, the throng of 90,000 people who gathered at the Alaska-Yukon-Pacific Exposition grounds in Seattle on June 1 to watch the opening of the newest world's fair reminded one very naturally of a millionaire gold miner and his first automobile.

— *R. S. Jones, Jr.,* What the Visitor Sees at the Seattle Fair, *1909*

Today there are nearly six million Washingtonians. About 83 percent live in metropolitan areas, most of which are in the Puget Sound Lowland. In fact, more than 50 percent live in the Seattle and Tacoma areas alone. East of the Cascades, most live in and around Spokane. They come from a diverse range of backgrounds and cultures. Washington has a relatively small percentage of African Americans, but it ranks among the top ten states in numbers of Native Americans and Asians.

Indigenous Washingtonians

By the end of the nineteenth century, most of Washington's Native Americans, representing three principal tribal groups — Coast Salish, Interior Salish, and Sahaptin — had been settled on reservations. Within these groups are

Age Distribution in Washington

0–4	394,306
5–19	1,288,713
20–24	390,185
25–44	1,816,217
45–64	1,342,552
65 and over	662,148

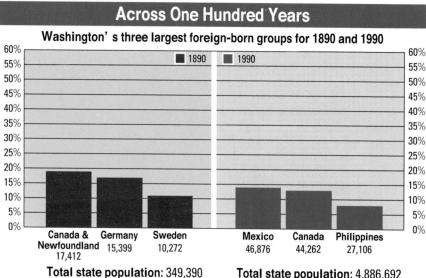

Across One Hundred Years

Washington's three largest foreign-born groups for 1890 and 1990

■ 1890 ■ 1990

| Canada & Newfoundland 17,412 | Germany 15,399 | Sweden 10,272 | Mexico 46,876 | Canada 44,262 | Philippines 27,106 |

Total state population: 349,390
Total foreign-born: 90,005 (25%)

Total state population: 4,886,692
Total foreign-born: 322,144 (7%)

Patterns of Immigration

The total number of people who immigrated to Washington in 1998 was 16,920. Of that number, the largest immigrant groups were from Mexico (24%), El Salvador (9%), and the Philippines (7%).

many distinct tribes. Among the larger tribes of western Washington are the Makah, Quinault, Lummi, Snohomish, and Puyallup. Tribes of eastern Washington include the Okanogan, Yakima, Klickitat, Kalispel, and Spokane.

Working on the Railroad

Ethnic diversity in Washington is partly a result of the policies of the Northern Pacific Railroad and Great

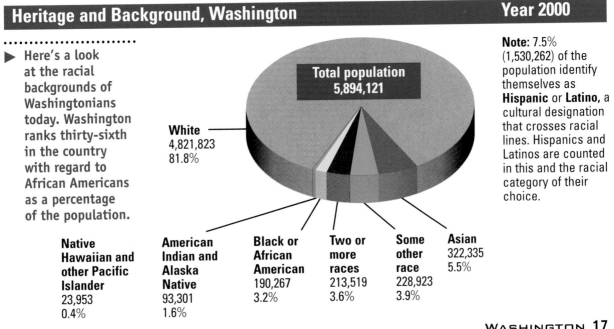

Heritage and Background, Washington — **Year 2000**

▶ Here's a look at the racial backgrounds of Washingtonians today. Washington ranks thirty-sixth in the country with regard to African Americans as a percentage of the population.

Total population 5,894,121

Note: 7.5% (1,530,262) of the population identify themselves as **Hispanic** or **Latino,** a cultural designation that crosses racial lines. Hispanics and Latinos are counted in this and the racial category of their choice.

White 4,821,823 81.8%

Native Hawaiian and other Pacific Islander 23,953 0.4%

American Indian and Alaska Native 93,301 1.6%

Black or African American 190,267 3.2%

Two or more races 213,519 3.6%

Some other race 228,923 3.9%

Asian 322,335 5.5%

Northern Railway companies. They encouraged the employment of Chinese construction workers in Washington, opening the way for other ethnic groups to follow. The many coal companies needed to keep the trains running brought in African-American miners from the East. Immigrants came from around the world — especially Britain, Italy, Russia, and Sweden — to work the farms and factories that cropped up between 1883 and 1920. In 1910 half of Washington's population was foreign-born.

In the 1920s the United States imposed quotas on foreign immigration, which cut down on the number of immigrants into Washington. However, significant numbers of foreign-born people still entered the state, especially from Canada and the Scandinavian countries. It was not until

Educational Levels of Washington Workers

Less than 9th grade	171,311
9th to 12th grade, no diploma	334,472
High school graduate, including equivalency	873,150
Some college, no degree	782,010
Associate degree	248,478
Bachelor's degree	496,866
Graduate or professional degree	220,103

▼ The skyline of Seattle, Washington's most populous city.

the 1950s that childbirth finally became a larger factor in Washington's population increase than immigration.

Wartime Hysteria

The Japanese also had a large immigrant population in Washington in the early part of the twentieth century. Shipowners and emigration companies recruited workers in Japan through advertisements in daily newspapers that depicted the United States as a golden land. Most Japanese immigrants entered through Seattle and Tacoma on Puget Sound.

By 1930 the Japanese population numbered about eighteen thousand. During World War II, however — whether U.S. citizens or not — they were moved from the coastal areas to relocation camps in inland regions. After the attack on Pearl Harbor, U.S. citizens, including many government officials in Washington, had become convinced that Japanese Americans were spies for Japan. In 1942 President Franklin Roosevelt ordered all people of Japanese descent out of the Pacific Northwest. Thousands of Japanese Americans were rounded up in Washington, taken to a center in Puyallup, and then sent to internment camps in California and Idaho. They were held there for the remainder of the war. After the war only a few had their homes and property returned. Many chose to live elsewhere. In 1988 the U.S. government finally apologized to the surviving internees and offered a symbolic payment of twenty thousand dollars to compensate for suffering and property lost while in internment camps.

Religious Diversity

Although the majority of Washingtonians (77 percent) are Christian, there is significant religious diversity in the state. Washington has the nation's largest population (1.4 percent) of agnostics — people who neither believe nor disbelieve in God. Most of the Christians in the state belong to one of a number of Protestant churches. Washington Protestants may be Baptists, Episcopalians, Jehovah's Witnesses, Lutherans, Pentecostals, Presbyterians, or Methodists, among many options. About 0.5 percent of the religiously affiliated population practices Buddhism, while 0.6 percent are Jewish and 3.2 percent are Catholic.

▲ Seattle's Pike Place Market. Seattle residents buy fresh fish, fruits, and vegetables from Pike Place Market on the waterfront. The market was opened in 1907 in response to outrage over rising produce costs. At Pike Place farmers and shoppers bypass the middleman.

More Coastline than Coast

> Great joy in camp, we are in view of the Ocean, this great Pacific Ocean, which we been so long anxious to see and the roreing or noise made by the waves . . . may be heard distinctly.
>
> — *Meriwether Lewis, November 1805*

Washington divides neatly into three regions: the coast in the west, the plains or plateau in the east, and the spine of mountains that divides them. It is the farthest north and farthest west of the forty-eight contiguous states. Its highest point is Mt. Rainier in the Cascade Mountains, which rises to 14,410 feet (4,392 meters). The Cascade Range creates such a vast barrier that the weather on each side is very different.

Climate

Although the western part of Washington is notoriously rainy, this is only partly supported by the statistics. Many places in the nation, for example, have greater rainfall than Seattle. Western Washington also has a much milder climate than any other part of the United States that far north. The annual precipitation on the Pacific slopes of the Olympic Peninsula and in the Cascades, however, can exceed 150 inches (381 centimeters). East of the Cascade Range, seasonal temperature variations are greater, but the Rocky Mountains shield the region from cold Canadian air masses in winter.

▼ *From left to right:* Boats on Lake Union; a lighthouse at sunset; Steptoe Butte State Park; a log cabin in Jackson; a tulip nursery; farmland with a view of the mountains.

Plant and Animal Life

Washington is home to 23,000,000 acres (9,308,000 hectares) of forest, the largest remaining forests in the United States. The forests are filled with Douglas fir, hemlock, western red cedar, Sitka spruce, yew, and ponderosa pine. Some of these trees grow very tall. Douglas firs can grow to a height of 300 feet (91 m) — only the sequoias of California are taller. In the dryer Columbia Basin, the primary plants are grasses, sagebrush, and other scattered shrubs.

Deer, elk, bears, mountain goats, and pumas (cougars) are among Washington's large mammals. The forested regions are home to flying squirrels and red foxes. The Cascades are home to grizzly bears; the Olympics, to black bears.

Freshwater fish include trout, bass, grayling, and sturgeon. Five species of salmon swim up western Washington streams each year to spawn, although dams have created problems for salmon and no one is sure how long they will be able to continue their age-old routine.

Islands

Although Washington only has about 150 miles (241 km) of coast along the Pacific Ocean, the state actually has much more coastline. The Strait of Juan de Fuca (south of Vancouver Island) and the Strait of Georgia (east of Vancouver Island) are both tidal shore, as is the complex system of waterways known as Puget Sound. These contribute to Washington's more than 3,000 miles (4,828 km) of coastline!

Another feature that adds to Washington's shoreline are the San Juan Islands. When the tide is out, almost eight hundred rocks and small areas of land can be called islands. When the tide comes in, about two hundred of

Average January temperature
Seattle: 39.4° F (4.1° C)
Spokane: 27.0° F (-2.8° C)

Average July temperature
Seattle: 64.6° F (18.1° C)
Spokane: 69.6° F (20.9 C)

Average yearly rainfall
Seattle: 34.5 in. (88 cm)
Spokane: 17.5 in. (44 cm)

Average yearly snowfall
Seattle: 11.4 in. (29 cm)
Spokane: 48.9 in. (124 cm)

DID YOU KNOW?

When it comes to snowfall, Mt. Baker in Washington State is king of the hill. Exactly 1,140 inches (2,896 cm) — that's 95 feet (29 m) — of snow fell on the Mt. Baker Ski Area from July 1, 1998, through June 30, 1999. That's the largest snowfall ever measured in the United States and also the most that we're sure about anywhere in the world. The old record was held by Mt. Rainier, also in Washington State.

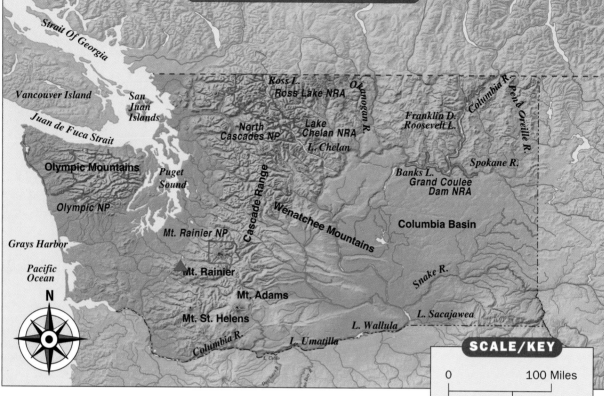

SCALE/KEY

0	100 Miles
0	100 Kilometers

NRA	National Resource Area
NP	National Park
▲	Highest Point
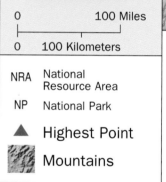	Mountains

them remain visible. The three largest of these islands are San Juan, Orcas, and Lopez. The islands are a good place to watch orcas ("killer whales") swimming in groups known as pods.

Rivers

The largest river in Washington, the Columbia River, is the second largest in the United States in terms of volume of water. The river makes a huge S-curve through the state of Washington and travels a total of 1,214 miles (1,954 km). Its largest tributary is the Snake River. These two rivers have very steep banks in many places, and their waters often flow far below the level of the surrounding land. Many former rapids have been tamed by dams. Some people believe the river has now been overtamed.

Lakes and Dams

She winds down her granite canyon and she bends across the lea
Like a silver running stallion down her seaway to the sea

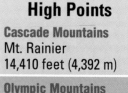

High Points

Cascade Mountains
Mt. Rainier
14,410 feet (4,392 m)

Olympic Mountains
Mt. Olympus
7,965 feet (2,428 m)

Cast your eye upon the great thing yet built by human hands
On the King Columbia River, it's that big Grand Coulee Dam.
— Folksinger Woody Guthrie

Eastern Washington was mostly desert until the Grand Coulee Dam was built in the 1930s. Its walls stand 550 feet (167 m). It is almost one mile (1.6 km) long. Behind the dam, Franklin D. Roosevelt Lake — actually the Columbia River, widened artificially by the dam — stretches for 150 miles (241 km). The Grand Coulee Dam is the largest concrete structure in the United States.

The dam's twenty-four generators produce 6.5 million kilowatts of electricity, making it the largest single source of power in the Northwest. From there, water is piped into Banks Lake and through pipes to irrigate about 500,000 acres (202,339 ha) of farmland.

Dams and Salmon

The Pacific Northwest is known for its salmon. There are five species of Pacific salmon — sockeye, Chinook, coho, chum, and pink — and people have been hunting and eating them for thousands of years.

Salmon hatch in freshwater rivers, then swim to the ocean, grow large, and eventually return to the freshwater of their birth to spawn (lay eggs) before dying. By some amazing instinct tiny, newly-hatched salmon ("fingerlings") know to swim to the ocean. Even more amazing, when they are grown, the salmon know how to swim back home — upstream! When rivers are dammed, however, adult salmon cannot reach their spawning grounds, and fingerlings cannot reach the sea because the giant turbines that produce electricity chew them into bits.

In recent years fish ladders have been added to the dams. Fish ladders are special areas designed for fish to swim through. Unfortunately, the foaming water often takes in more nitrogen than the fish can stand, and many salmon die in the fish ladders. Today no one is certain how to balance the region's need for irrigation and energy generation with the desire to protect the endangered salmon species.

Major Rivers

Columbia River
1,240 miles (2,000 km) long

Snake River
1,040 miles (1,670 km) long. From elevations of 10,000 feet (3,000 m), the river descends to 300 feet (90 m).

Spokane River
100 miles (160 km) long; 50 miles (80 km) in Washington

Largest Lakes

Lake Chelan
55 miles (88.5 km) long

Lake Washington
4 miles (6.4 km) at widest point; 13 miles (21 km) long; 50 square miles (80.5 sq km)

▼ The Grand Coulee Dam.

From Fur to Software

> Will you permit . . . this Bureau earnestly to request you to urge upon . . . your employees, that they should at once proceed to correspond with their old home newspapers and with friends in the East setting forth the merits of Seattle as the best Alaskan outfitting point. . . .
>
> — *Erastus Brainerd, Seattle Chamber of Commerce, 1897*

Washington's oldest industries are agriculture, forestry, and fishing. These have been the state's prominent industries since its earliest inhabitants settled there. In the last half-century, though, manufacturing and other businesses have been on the rise. More and more Washingtonians have settled in urban areas.

Resources

Washington's most valuable and most versatile natural resource is water. Its biggest source of freshwater is the Columbia River, from which a series of dams collects water for irrigation and hydroelectric power. Hydroelectric power is electricity generated by the flow of water. There are more than one thousand dams on rivers in Washington. The Columbia and other rivers of Washington account for one-third of all hydroelectric production in the United States.

Washington also has more acres of forest than any other state. Its forests support both wood-product industries (like logging and lumber processing) and a sizeable wildlife population. Today the people of Washington work to use their forests sustainably, meaning that trees are harvested with minimum damage to the environment and also that at least as many trees are allowed to grow as are cut down. This way the industry and the forests can both exist for future generations.

Commercial fisheries are another major element of the state's economy. Salmon, halibut, cod, and herring are the

DID YOU KNOW?

The Native American Makah nation on the Washington coast are the only people in the United States with government permission to hunt whales — because it is an ancestral tradition for them.

Top Employers
(of workers age sixteen and over)

Service industries (dry cleaners, restaurants, etc.) 26.6%

Wholesale and retail trade 24.7%

Manufacturing . .14.2%

Transportation and public utilities . . .5.1%

Finance, insurance, and real estate . .5.2%

Construction 5.2%

Federal, state, and local government (including military) 19.0%

Mining 0.1%

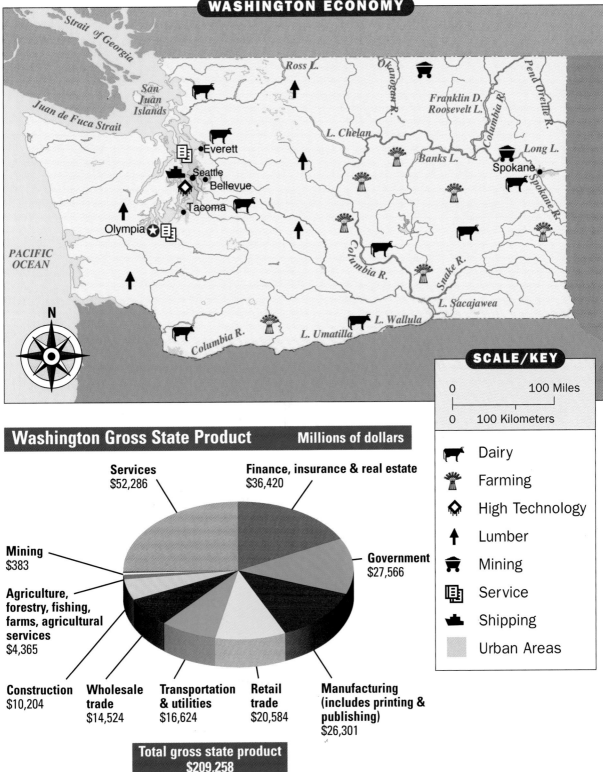

WASHINGTON ECONOMY

Strait of Georgia
Ross L.
Okanogan R.
Franklin D. Roosevelt L.
Pend Oreille R.
San Juan Islands
L. Chelan
Banks L.
Columbia R.
Long L.
Spokane
Juan de Fuca Strait
• Everett
Seattle
Bellevue
Spokane R.
• Tacoma
Olympia
PACIFIC OCEAN
Columbia R.
Snake R.
L. Sacajawea
L. Wallula
Columbia R.
L. Umatilla

N

SCALE/KEY

| 0 | 100 Miles |
| 0 | 100 Kilometers |

🐄 Dairy
🌾 Farming
◈ High Technology
↑ Lumber
⛏ Mining
🗎 Service
⚓ Shipping
▨ Urban Areas

Washington Gross State Product — Millions of dollars

Services $52,286

Finance, insurance & real estate $36,420

Mining $383

Government $27,566

Agriculture, forestry, fishing, farms, agricultural services $4,365

Construction $10,204

Wholesale trade $14,524

Transportation & utilities $16,624

Retail trade $20,584

Manufacturing (includes printing & publishing) $26,301

Total gross state product $209,258

principal species landed at ports on Grays Harbor, Willapa Bay, and Puget Sound. Salmon, trout, and shellfish are also farmed in special aquaculture farms.

Agriculture

Winter wheat is the state's leading crop and a major export from the Columbia Basin, where barley, dry peas, lentils, and hay are also grown. Irrigated crops include potatoes, vegetables, fruits, hops, and mint. Washington produces more apples than any other state. It is also a major producer of pears, cranberries, and wine grapes. In the Puget Sound Lowland, farmers grow vegetables, berries, and flower bulbs. This region is also known for its dairy and poultry farms.

Farms vary from a few acres to thousands of acres. Since the 1900s the tendency has been toward larger and fewer farms. Also, former farms near cities are being turned into suburbs at a very fast pace.

Manufacturing

In the nineteenth century Washington's factories primarily made products using the state's raw materials, especially wood. By the middle of the twentieth century, however,

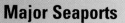

Major Seaports

- **Seattle,** on Elliott Bay — the fourth largest container port in the United States

- **Tacoma,** on Commencement Bay — the sixth largest container port in the United States

- **Grays Harbor** — the only deepwater port on Washington's coast

▼ *From left to right:* **Logs destined for a lumber mill; the Boeing 777 being assembled.**

Washington's major manufacturing industry became airplanes — thanks to the Boeing Company. Boeing was founded in 1916 by William E. Boeing and his partner G. Conrad Westerveldt. They used native spruce wood to build airplanes. After World War I, Boeing built airplanes for carrying mail. It also started an airline — United — the first to have flight attendants. The government, however, required Boeing to split up the company, and United Airlines became its own company.

Today Boeing employs about seventy-eight thousand workers in Washington but has moved its corporate headquarters to Chicago, Illinois. Remaining in Everett, Washington, is the Boeing Commercial Airplane Factory, the largest building in the world. It covers almost 100 acres (41 ha) or roughly one hundred baseball fields, and workers ride bicycles to get around inside it.

A number of prominent national businesses were founded in Seattle, including clothing retailer Eddie Bauer, coffee chain Starbucks, and gaming company Wizards of the Coast (creators of the Magic: The Gathering collectible card game).

Perhaps the most important business located in Washington today is Microsoft. The company was founded by Bill Gates and Paul Allen, both native Washingtonians. They went from developing computer languages in their college dorm rooms to designing a language and operating system for IBM in 1980. This was called MS-DOS, which later developed into Windows. Windows is now used on about 90 percent of the world's personal computers, such a large percentage that Microsoft was declared a monopoly in court. Microsoft became the fastest-growing technology company in history. Bill Gates is the world's richest person.

Tourism is also a major source of income in Washington. The variety of scenic areas — including three national parks — draws increasing numbers of visitors to the state. Boating, hiking, skiing, sports events, and local festivals are other major tourist attractions.

▲ Washington's most famous export.

Made in Washington

Leading Farm Products and Crops
Wheat
Apples
Cherries
Cranberries
Plums
Grapes
Pears
Blueberries
Flower bulbs
Fish

Other Products
Coal
Lumber and wood products
Transportation equipment, especially aircraft and aerospace equipment
Computer software

International Airports		
Airport	Location	Passengers per Year (2000)
Seattle-Tacoma International	Seattle	28,408,553
Spokane International	Spokane	3,068,242

A State of Progress

THE SEAL OF THE STATE OF WASHINGTON 1889

> The Seattle General Strike [of February 1919] was not a revolution, but it was a revolt — a revolt against everything and therefore a revolt against nothing.
> — *Robert L. Friedheim, "The Seattle General Strike of 1919," 1961*

Making a State

Until the 1840s citizens of both the United States and Britain could settle and trade in what was still known as the Oregon Country. In 1846 the two countries agreed on a boundary between the United States and Canada at the forty-ninth parallel. In 1848 the U.S. Congress established Oregon Territory, including all of what is now Oregon, Washington, and Idaho, plus parts of Wyoming and Montana.

The Territory covered roughly 250,000 square miles (647,500 square kilometers). Such a large area was difficult to govern, and people clamored to form a separate territory in the area north and west of the Columbia River. In 1853 Congress created the Washington Territory — named for the first president of the United States — and extended it east of the Columbia River to the crest of the Rocky Mountains, including parts of present-day Idaho and Montana.

Between 1867 and 1889 Washington Territory repeatedly asked for statehood. Each time the U.S. Congress refused to grant the request. Finally, on November 11, 1889, Washington was admitted to the Union as the forty-second state. Washington is governed under its original constitution adopted in 1889, as amended.

Political History

Washington's government, like the nation's, is divided into three branches — the executive, judicial, and legislative. However, not everything about these branches is exactly like their national counterparts.

The state has been progressive almost since the start of

Washington State Constitution

All political power is inherent in the people, and governments derive their just powers from the consent of the governed, and are established to protect and maintain individual rights.

"Declaration of Rights," from the Washington State Constitution.

Top Elected Posts in the Executive Branch		
Office	Length of Term	Term Limits
Governor	4 years	2 terms
Lieutenant Governor	4 years	2 terms
Secretary of State	4 years	2 terms
Attorney General	4 years	2 terms

its history. This means that citizens are often willing to enact political changes before they have become popular in the rest of the nation. In 1910, for example, Washington voters approved a state constitutional amendment that gave women the right to vote. That was ten years before the United States passed a similar national amendment. The state legislature had actually granted women the right to vote during Territory days but was overruled by the courts.

In state and local politics, Washington has been a two-party state. Democrats and Republicans have often alternated in the governorship. In presidential elections Washington voters generally favored Republican candidates before 1932, then backed Democrat Franklin D. Roosevelt in his four races (1932–1944), and thereafter reverted to Republicans. Washington sends two senators and nine representatives to the U.S. Congress and casts eleven electoral votes in presidential elections.

Executive Branch

Perhaps because it was a western frontier state far from the federal government, Washington State's founders had a strong distrust of government. Washington's constitution of 1889 reflected that distrust in its many restrictions on state power. One result of this was the creation of a divided executive branch. Unlike the federal executive branch, to which only the president and vice president are elected, the state has nine separately elected officials. The most important of

▼ The Washington State Capitol building was completed in 1928. Of all the state capitol buildings, it matches the architecture of the U.S. Capitol Building, in Washington, D.C., most closely.

these is the governor, but the governor does not have complete power over the executive branch.

The Legislature

Washington's government has a powerful system of checks and balances. Voters *check* the legislature by having the power to create referendums to change legislation or recall elected officials. The governor checks the legislature with his or her line-item veto, which allows the governor to veto individual lines in legislation. The Washington legislature is bicameral, which means that it has two houses. This provides a further check on government power because both houses have to agree to pass a law.

A bill may be introduced in either house. A committee studies the bill and often holds public hearings on it. A report from the committee is read in an open session, and the bill is then referred to the rules committee. The rules committee can either place the bill on the calendar for a second reading and debate before the entire body, or it can take no action. At the second reading a bill is subject to debate and amendment before being placed on the calendar for a third reading and final passage. After passing one house the bill goes through the same procedure in the other house. If amendments are made in one house, the other house must agree. When the bill is accepted by both houses, it is signed by the respective house leaders and sent to the governor.

▲ A view of the Washington legislature from the gallery.

The Judicial System

Washington's courts are divided into four levels. District and municipal courts deal with misdemeanor criminal cases, traffic cases, domestic violence protection orders, and civil actions of $50,000 or less. Superior courts — with a total of 159 judges — deal with larger civil cases, domestic relations, felony criminal cases, and juvenile matters. The superior

Legislature			
House	Number of Members	Length of Term	Term Limits
Senate	49 senators	4 years	2 terms
House of Representatives	98 representatives	2 years	3 terms

courts also hear appeals from the lower courts. An appeal is when one party in a case is dissatisfied with a decision and asks a higher court to review it. The right of appeal is crucial to our legal system because it ensures that judges are not "above the law." The court of appeals consists of seventeen judges and hears appeals from the superior courts. Finally, the highest court in the state, the Washington Supreme Court, decides any appeals from court of appeals.

The supreme court consists of a chief justice and eight associate justices. Its opinions are published, become the laws of the state, and set precedent for subsequent cases decided in Washington. This means that the decision of the supreme court in any given appeal can be called upon to help settle future cases. Its decisions can be appealed only to the United States Supreme Court in Washington, D.C.

The nine supreme court justices in Washington State are elected to six-year terms on a ballot with no party affiliations. Their terms are staggered so the justices are not all voted in at the same time. The only requirement for the office is that the prospective justice be admitted to the practice of law in Washington State.

Local Government

Washington has a strong tradition of local government dating back to its territorial days before statehood. There are two "general-purpose" local governments in Washington State: counties and cities. There are 39 counties and 280 cities. The key distinction between counties and cities is in the territory covered. In most cases county governments cover larger land areas than do city governments that are established to govern concentrated urban areas. While city boundaries can change, counties are permanent areas of the state.

Beginning shortly after statehood, the legislature also authorized new units of government known as "special purpose districts" to provide specific services to defined populations. As the years went by, more special purpose districts were created, some providing city-type services (such as fire, water, and sewer) to people living in noncity areas.

▼ The streets of Seattle were in chaos in November 2000 when thousands of people protested the World Trade Organization (WTO) meeting. This scene shows a crowd member near Westlake Park.

Potlatch on the Pacific

> Something wild and free, something robust and full will come out of the West and be recognized in the final American type. Under the shadow of those great mountains a distinct personality shall arise, it shall adopt other fashions, create new ideals, and generations shall justify them.
>
> — *Adell M. Parker, president of the alumni association of the University of Washington, 1894*

A cultural practice associated with the Native Americans around Washington State was the *potlatch,* a ceremonial distribution of gifts to show social status. Great formalities were shown in inviting guests, making speeches, feasting, and distributing gifts. The size of the gatherings reflected the rank of the donor. Important events such as marriages, births, deaths, and initiations were occasions for potlatches, but even trivial events could be celebrated.

The Chinook people held a ritual called the First Salmon Rite, which welcomed the annual salmon run — when the salmon return upstream to spawn. Another important cultural rite was the spirit quest, an ordeal undertaken by boys and girls to find guardian spirits that would give them hunting, healing, or other powers, bring them good luck, or teach them songs and dances.

Today a vibrant Native American culture survives amidst an increasingly diverse population. Washington has earned a reputation as a maverick state, enjoying its position at a far corner of the nation. That distance and relative isolation have given it the freedom to do things its own way. More than most other states, it has tended toward radicalism in politics and culture. Perhaps the most pervasive elements determining the character of the state, however, have been a relaxed pace of life and a philosophy of harmony with the natural environment.

Different regions host different kinds of events —

DID YOU KNOW?

A neighborhood of Seattle was the first ever to be called *skid row.* Trees were logged on the hills around town and moved downhill to the waterfront by skidding them along greased tracks. These skids ran along Yesler Way in downtown Seattle. The road attracted all kinds of people, many of them up to no good. Today skid row refers to the worst parts of cities all around the world.

agricultural fairs, blossom festivals, parades, you name it! Bellingham is home to an annual Chalk Art Festival, where people of all ages decorate the city's sidewalks with chalk — and hope it doesn't rain! The annual Seattle Seafair features parades, boat races, and water carnivals. In eastern Washington rodeos preserve memories of the days when cattle ranching was a major local industry. Many of the ethnic groups in Washington hold festivals to celebrate the food, dance, and music of their places of origin.

▲ The Folklife Festival, Seattle.

Music

Seattle is truly renowned for its music. The Seattle Symphony Orchestra and Seattle Opera are both respected around the world. Music festivals of all kinds are held throughout the state. The city of Seattle has even become synonymous with a style of rock music known as grunge, which emerged in the Pacific Northwest during the late 1980s and changed the course of popular music in the 1990s. The grunge hybrid of punk and heavy metal was

Indian Princess

One of the daughters of Chief Sealth was Princess Angeline, who lived out her old age in a waterfront shack in downtown Seattle. She gained fame as the subject of photographs taken by Edward S. Curtis (1868–1925). Curtis went on to become the most famous early photographer of Native Americans. He devoted his life to photographing Native Americans throughout the United States.

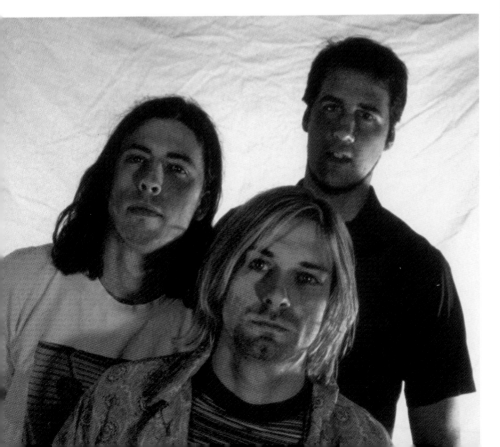

◄ Grunge band Nirvana.

defined in the clubs of Seattle by bands like Nirvana, Pearl Jam, Mudhoney, and Soundgarden. With the music came a distinctive youth culture. Fans around the world grieved at the death of Nirvana's Kurt Cobain in 1994, just as a generation earlier their parents had grieved the early death of another Washingtonian, Jimi Hendrix, who helped define his own era by revolutionizing the playing of the electric guitar.

Museums

Native American totem poles can be seen throughout the state, especially in Seattle. The Seattle Art Museum displays art from around the world, as well as a major collection of regional Native American art. Other museums include the Seattle Asian Art Museum, the Thomas Burke Memorial Washington State Museum, and the Museum of History and Industry. Seattle has about twenty-five major museums and art galleries in all.

Parks

Washington State has three national parks and more than 125 state parks. Places to visit include Mt. Rainier National Park, the Columbia River Gorge National Scenic Area, the Mount St. Helens National Volcanic Monument, Colville National Forest, North Cascades National Park, Gifford Pinchot National Forest, Okanogan National Forest, Olympic National Forest, Hanford

◀ This "sound sculpture" entitled *If VI was IX* was designed by Seattle artist Trimpin. The sculpture is part of the Experience Music Project (EMP).

SEATTLE CHILDREN'S THEATRE

FLIGHT

A LIVING NEWSPAPER PLAY · · ·

MARCH
5·12·19
2:00 P·M·

CHILDREN 10¢
ADULTS 20¢

FEDERAL THEATRE
RAINIER & ATLANTIC

◀ A Works Progress Administration (WPA) poster for a children's play in Seattle, circa 1936.

STATE GREATS

Washington State has given birth to popular artists of all eras.

▶ **Gypsy Rose Lee** (1914–1970) was an international burlesque sensation.

▶ **Bing Crosby** (1903–1977) and his brother Bob helped define the crooner era of popular music from the 1930s to the 1950s.

▶ **Judy Collins** (born 1939) was influential in the coffeehouse folk scene of the 1960s.

▶ **Jimi Hendrix** (1942–1970) was one of the icons of psychedelic rock in the late 1960s.

▶ **Kurt Cobain** (1967–1994) and other Washingtonians helped define the grunge sound that was closely identified with the city of Seattle before sweeping the world in the early 1990s.

Reach National Monument, Olympic National Park, Hoh/Quinault Rain Forests, the Hell's Canyon National Recreation Area, Umatilla National Forest, Mt. Baker–Snoqualmie National Forest, and Wenatchee National Forest.

The deepest gorge in North America — Hell's Canyon on the Snake River — is several thousand feet deeper than the Grand Canyon. Visitors can float on rafts through the central section of the river. On sunny days Mt. Rainier can be seen from downtown Seattle as an enormous snowy cone on the horizon. The mountain is a massive volcano with a vertical rise from the surrounding plateau equal to the tallest mountains on Earth. Visitors can hike trails through ancient forests and gaze at glaciers while standing amidst a sea of wildflowers.

Sports

Sports are an important part of life in Washington. Many people support college football teams, including the University of Washington Huskies and the Washington State Cougars. The Huskies won their fourth Rose Bowl game in 2001. The Cougars played in the Rose Bowl in 1998 for the first time since 1931.

The state is also home to several major-league sports teams. Washington's National Basketball Association (NBA) team is the Seattle SuperSonics. They began playing in

Sport	Team	Home
Baseball	Seattle Mariners	Safeco Field, Seattle
Basketball	Seattle SuperSonics	KeyArena, Seattle
Women's Basketball	Seattle Storm	KeyArena, Seattle
Football	Seattle Seahawks	Seahawks Stadium, Seattle
Hockey	Seattle Thunderbirds	KeyArena, Seattle
Soccer	Seattle Sounders	Memorial Stadium, Seattle

DID YOU KNOW?

The Seattle Pilots baseball team joined the American League in 1969 but by the next year were already reborn as the Milwaukee Brewers. The Pilots were the first major league baseball team to declare bankruptcy and only the second in the twentieth century to move after just a single season. Low attendance was one of the reasons for their problems. So it's strange that interest in the Pilots is now much greater than it was when the team existed. Pitcher Jim Bouton wrote of his experience with the team in what is now a classic baseball book, *Ball Four*.

▼ Windsurfers on the Columbia River in Maryhill State Park.

1967 and won the NBA championship once, in 1979. The state's Women's National Basketball Association (WNBA) team is the Seattle Storm. The state's National Football League (NFL) team is the Seattle Seahawks, founded in 1976. They won a division championship in 1988 but have never made it to the Super Bowl. The state's soccer team is the Seattle Sounders. Washington's major league baseball team is the Seattle Mariners, founded in 1977.

Water sports are popular on many lakes and rivers and especially on Puget Sound. Skiing is a favorite winter sport in the Cascades and Okanogan Highlands.

Education

In 1859 Rev. Cushing Eells founded Whitman Seminary in Walla Walla as a memorial to an earlier missionary, Dr. Marcus Whitman. It was the first college chartered by territorial legislation, but it closed and reopened several times before becoming Whitman College in 1883.

▲ The Washington Huskies at play.

The University of Washington opened in Seattle in 1861 with one building, one teacher, and one student! By 1881 the legislature was funding the school, which helped it grow rapidly. In 1909 the university claimed buildings that had been constructed for the Alaska–Yukon–Pacific Exposition. Today it has campuses in Bothell, Seattle, and Tacoma and serves about thirty-five thousand students at its Seattle campus alone.

Other universities in Washington include Washington State University (originally an agricultural college), Western Washington University, and Eastern and Central Washington Universities.

High Flyers

We arrived in Seattle on a June day. My first sight of the approaching land was an exhilarating experience . . . With a sudden surge of joy, I knew that I must find a home in this new land.

— *Carlos Bulosan*, America Is in the Heart: A Personal History, *1943*

Following are only a few of the thousands of people who lived, died, or spent most of their lives in Washington and made extraordinary contributions to the state and the nation.

CHIEF JOSEPH

NATIVE AMERICAN CHIEF

BORN: *about 1840, Wallowa Valley, Oregon Territory*
DIED: *September 21, 1904, Colville Reservation*

Although early settlers knew this Nez Percé chief as Chief Joseph, his real name was In-mut-too-yah-lat-lat. He signed a treaty agreeing to move to a reservation in Idaho, but when he learned that three young Native Americans had killed a band of white settlers, he feared retaliation and decided instead to lead his 250 warriors and their families to Canada. They then spent more than three months holding off U.S. troops. He won much admiration for his humane treatment of prisoners and concern for women and children. He also purchased supplies from ranchers and storekeepers rather than steal them. On October 5, 1877, Chief Joseph finally surrendered to General Nelson Miles.

Miles had cornered Joseph and his followers in Montana's Bear Paw Mountains, close to the Canadian border. When he surrendered, Joseph made this speech:

Hear me, my chiefs; my heart is sick and sad. Our chiefs are dead, the little children are freezing. My people have no blankets, no food. From where the Sun now stands, I will fight no more forever.

Chester F. Carlson
INVENTOR

BORN: *February 8, 1906, Seattle*
DIED: *September 19, 1968, New York, NY*

As a fourteen-year-old, Carlson published a chemistry magazine to help provide for his parents, both in poor health. His early interest in chemistry paid off. After obtaining a degree in physics from the California Institute of Technology, he began working in the patent office at an electronics company. Deluged with paperwork, Carlson recognized the need for a way to copy documents quickly. Unlike other scientists at the time, he decided that the method should not rely on wet photographic chemicals but on "dry" ink charged with electricity. He received a patent in 1940 for the first "dry-copy" process, using electrostatics. Eighteen years later, in 1958, the Xerox Corporation introduced the first photocopier, which was based primarily on Carlson's work.

Mary McCarthy
WRITER

BORN *June 21, 1912, Seattle*
DIED *October 25, 1989, New York, NY*

When she was six years old, both of Mary McCarthy's parents died in a flu epidemic, and she was then reared by her grandparents. McCarthy went to school at the Annie Wright Seminary in Tacoma and then at Vassar College, where she studied literature and met famous writers such as Elizabeth Bishop. She became a writer and theater critic noted for her satirical commentaries on marriage, intellectuals, and the role of women in modern society. McCarthy's novels were often drawn from autobiographical sources. Her best-selling novel, *The Group,* was about her classmates at Vassar and their lives.

Frank Herbert
WRITER

BORN: *October 8, 1920, Tacoma*
DIED: *February 11, 1986, Madison, WI*

Frank Herbert was a science-fiction writer best known for his *Dune* series of futuristic novels set on the planet of Arakis. The first *Dune* book was published in 1965 and has now sold over twelve million copies in fourteen languages. Five sequels followed, and more are now being written by Herbert's son Brian with his cowriter Kevin J. Anderson. As a lesson in perseverance, remember that the first *Dune* novel was originally rejected by twenty publishers!

ROBERT JOFFREY
BALLET DANCER
BORN: *December 24, 1930, Seattle*
DIED: *March 25, 1988, New York, NY*

Young Abdullah Jeffa Bey Kah was afflicted with asthma and at age six began tap dancing to improve his health. Soon he turned to ballet. His love of dance led him to move to New York in 1948 and join the School of American Ballet. He changed his name to Robert Joffrey and made his dancing premiere with a French dance company, Ballets de Paris, a year later. In 1952 Joffrey choreographed his first of many pieces, *Persephone*, based on the Greek myth. The next year he opened his own school of dance, the American Ballet Center, and also taught dance at New York City's High School of the Performing Arts. Eventually Joffrey moved his school to Chicago, where it is today known as the Joffrey Ballet of Chicago. Joffrey wanted the dances he choreographed to be accessible, using then-contemporary music such as the Beach Boys and other rock-and-roll and jazz tunes to appeal to wider audiences. He succeeded; his company and his work became nationally recognized and acclaimed during his lifetime.

JIMI HENDRIX
MUSICIAN
BORN: *November 27, 1942, Seattle*
DIED: *September 18, 1970, London, England*

John Allen Hendrix changed his name to James (nickname "Jimi") and became one of the great rock stars of his era. He was a guitarist, singer, and composer who incorporated elements of blues, jazz, rock, and soul into his music. He played the electric guitar in ways no one had ever thought possible. Although his musical career lasted only four years, Hendrix became one of the most influential rock musicians ever. He died in London, England, in 1970.

CAROLYN KIZER
POET
BORN: *December 10, 1925, Spokane*

Carolyn Kizer cofounded *Poetry Northwest* magazine in 1959, which she edited until 1965. After serving in Pakistan as literary specialist for the U.S. State Department from 1964 to 1970, she became the first director of literary programs for the National Endowment for the Arts. "Pro Femina," one of her best-known poems, is a satire about women writers. She was awarded the Pulitzer Prize for poetry in 1985 for her collection *Yin: New Poems*.

GARY LARSON
CARTOONIST

BORN: *August 14, 1950, Tacoma*

Gary Larson started drawing when he was a kid but gave it up in high school and concentrated on music and science instead. After college, while working in a music store, he drew six cartoons and submitted them to a local magazine. They were accepted and that was the beginning of his new career. In 1979 the *San Francisco Chronicle* decided to syndicate his cartoon *The Far Side.* That very same day, the *Seattle Times* decided to drop the cartoon, saying it was too offensive! After fifteen successful years with the comic strip, Larson stopped drawing it in 1995. Most recently he has published a children's book.

KURT COBAIN
MUSICIAN

BORN: *February 20, 1967, Aberdeen*
DIED: *April 5, 1994, Seattle*

Born in Aberdeen in 1967, Kurt Cobain was lead singer for the band Nirvana. Nirvana was the best known of the grunge rock bands who came to national attention in the late 1980s. The sound was dense, and the lyrics expressed the cynicism of Generation X, who came of age during an economic recession. Nirvana's album, *Nevermind,* released in 1991 and featuring the song "Smells Like Teen Spirit," made the band famous. Because grunge was inspired by distaste for commercialized rock music, fame and commercial success were uncomfortable for some grunge artists. When the group's next album, *In Utero,* became a number one hit, it was all too much for Cobain, and he killed himself in 1994 at the age of twenty-seven.

BILL GATES
ENTREPRENEUR

BORN: *October 28, 1955, Seattle*

Bill Gates is the son of a lawyer and a schoolteacher. He became interested in computers, along with his friend and future business partner Paul Allen, at the age of thirteen. Gates later dropped out of Harvard University to develop a computer language called BASIC. He and Allen started a software company and called it Microsoft. In 1980 they were asked to create an operating system for IBM. They called it MS-DOS, which eventually developed into the widely used Windows operating system. Today Gates is the richest person in the world.

Washington
History At-A-Glance

1592
Juan de Fuca sails the Washington shores.

1775
Bruno Heceta and Juan de Bodega y Quadra claim the land for Spain.

1778
James Cook explores and charts the Northwest coast.

1792
George Vancouver enters Puget Sound.

1792
Robert Gray explores the Columbia River.

1792
Spain establishes the first non-Indian settlement in Washington.

1805
Lewis and Clark travel through the Snake and Columbia Rivers to the Pacific Coast.

1824
Hudson Bay Company establishes Fort Vancouver for the trading of furs.

1846
Treaty between United States and Great Britain sets boundary between U.S. and Canada at 49th parallel.

1848
Cayuse War.

1848
Oregon Territory is established, including modern-day Oregon, Washington, and parts of Idaho.

1851
City of Seattle founded.

1600   **1700**   **1800**

1492
Christopher Columbus comes to New World.

1607
Capt. John Smith and three ships land on Virginia coast and start first English settlement in New World — Jamestown.

1754–63
French and Indian War.

1773
Boston Tea Party.

1776
Declaration of Independence adopted July 4.

1777
Articles of Confederation adopted by Continental Congress.

1787
U.S. Constitution written.

1812–14
War of 1812.

United States
History At-A-Glance

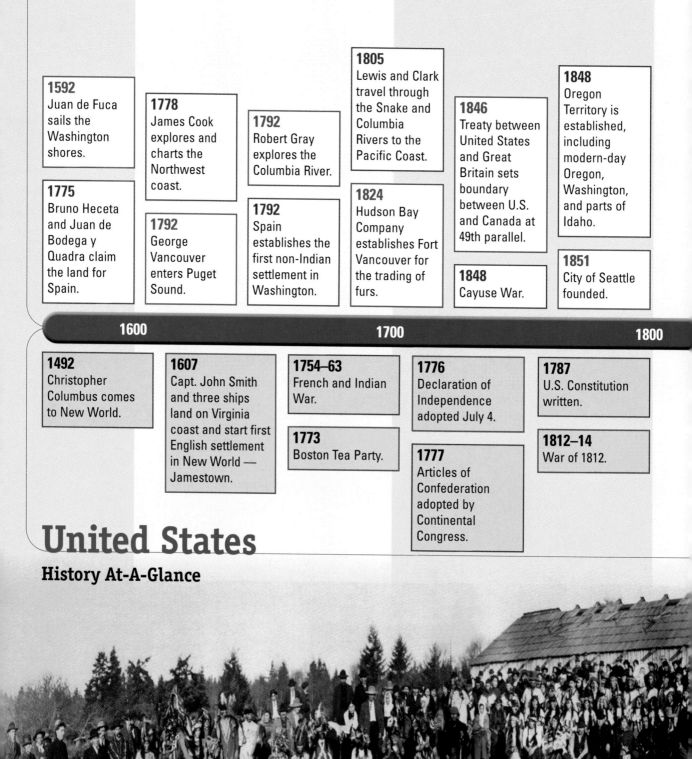

1980
Mt. St. Helens erupts.

1933
Grand Coulee Dam begun.

1889
Washington becomes 42nd state.

1910
Women gain the right to vote in Washington.

1942
Japanese-Americans removed from Washington and placed in camps until 1945.

1962
Seattle World's Fair.

1991
Collision of a Japanese fishing boat and a Chinese freighter covers the beaches of Olympic National Park with oil.

1855-1858
Yakima Wars.

1909
Alaska-Yukon-Pacific Exposition held in Seattle.

1919
Seattle general strike.

1978
Microsoft moves to Seattle.

1877
Nez Percé War.

1800   **1900**   **2000**

1848
Gold discovered in California draws 80,000 prospectors in the 1849 Gold Rush.

1869
Transcontinental Railroad completed.

1929
Stock market crash ushers in Great Depression.

1950–53
U.S. fights in the Korean War.

2000
George W. Bush wins the closest presidential election in history.

1917–18
U.S. involvement in World War I.

1941–45
U.S. involvement in World War II.

1964–73
U.S. involvement in Vietnam War.

1861–65
Civil War.

2001
A terrorist attack in which four hijacked airliners crash into New York City's World Trade Center, the Pentagon, and farmland in western Pennsylvania leaves thousands dead or injured.

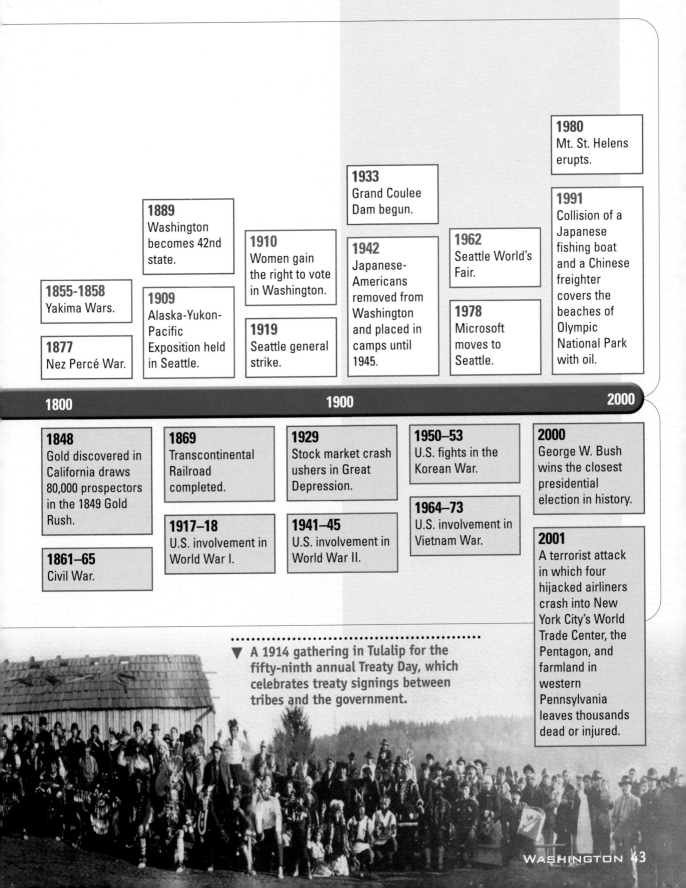

▼ A 1914 gathering in Tulalip for the fifty-ninth annual Treaty Day, which celebrates treaty signings between tribes and the government.

Festivals and Fun for All

Check web site for exact date and directions.

Apple Blossom Festival, Wenatchee

The oldest major festival in the state celebrates the fact that Washington is #1 in U.S. apple production.

www.appleblossom.org

Bellingham Festival of Music, Bellingham

A stellar mix of symphony orchestra, chamber music, jazz, and ethnic music is performed on a nightly basis during the festival each summer.

www.bellinghamfestival.org

Blackberry Festival, Bremerton

More than one hundred booths offer arts, crafts, and food — especially food featuring blackberries.

bremertonmainstreet.org/events/
blackberryfestival/index.html

Bumbershoot, Seattle

The often rainy city of Seattle sponsors a four-day arts festival showcasing umbrella art and great music.

www.bumbershoot.com

Central Washington State Fair, Yakima

This state fair features car racing and a rodeo!

www.yakima-herald.com/
fairfun/index.html

Daffodil Festival, Tacoma

Nearly seventy years old, this annual event features a Grand Floral Street Parade that travels through the cities of Tacoma, Puyallup, Sumner, and Orting, all in one day.

www.daffodilfestival.net

Clark County Fair, Ridgefield

Thousands of exhibits and animals, special attractions, contests, and a gigantic carnival and midway!

www.clarkcofair.com

Discovery Walk and Taste of Nations Festival, Vancouver

A walking festival designed to foster international friendship. Dozens of nations participate.

www.discoverywalk.org

Fremont Fair, Seattle

Celebrate summer along the streets of Seattle.

fremontfair.com

Foolproof, Seattle

Find out how laughter benefits health and community in a celebration of fun.

www.foolproof.org

The National Lentil Festival, **Pullman**

Honor the nutritious lentil at this fun-filled festival.

www.lentilfest.com

Northwest Folklife Festival, **Seattle**

Traditional music, dance, exhibits, demonstrations, and workshops.

www.nwfolklife.org

Salty Sea Days, **Everett**

A four-day blues festival, a celebration of Hawaiian culture, a carnival and midway, and more.

saltyseadays.org

Skagit Valley Tulip Festival, **Skagit County**

Flowers bloom during this fabulous festival.

www.tulipfestival.org

Washington State Square and Folk Dance Festival, **Longview**

Pioneers brought with them a dance called the *quadrille,* a French word that means "square." On April 17, 1979, the square dance became the official Washington State dance, and this festival celebrates that pioneer heritage.

www.squaredance-wa.org

Washington State International Kite Festival, **Long Beach**

A high-flying event with competitions, classes, and more.

www.kitefestival.com

▼ Kites fly in the Washington sky.

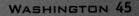

Books

Cone, Molly. *Come Back, Salmon: How a Group of Dedicated Kids Adopted Pigeon Creek and Brought it Back to Life.* San Francisco, CA: Sierra Club Juveniles, 1994. Kids just like you practice conservation.

Hodge, Deborah. *Whale: Killer Whales, Blue Whales and More.* Toronto, Ontario: The Kids Can Press Wildlife Series, 1997. Amazing information about the giants off Washington's shores.

Lauber, Patricia. *Volcano: The Eruption and Healing of Mt. St. Helens.* Minneapolis, MN: Econo-Clad Books, 1999. A U.S. natural disaster and its aftermath.

Marsh, Carole. *Washington State: Surprising Secrets About our State's Founding.* Peachtree City, GA: Gallopade Pub Group, 1996. A unique and timely title to help kids learn about extraordinary people in Washington's history.

Takami, David. *Divided Destiny: A History of Japanese Americans in Seattle.* Seattle, WA: Wing Luke Asian Museum Press, 1998. Learn about Japanese-American internment during World War II.

Web Sites

▶ Official state web site
www.state.wa.us

▶ Official site of the state's capital
www.ci.olympia.wa.us

▶ The Washington State Historical Society
www.wshs.org

▶ Killer Whale Tales
www.killerwhaletales.org
Ask scientists questions about killer whales or listen to real whale audio

▶ Center for Columbia River History
ccrh.org

▶ Volcano World
volcano.und.nodak.edu
Everything you need to know about Washington's volcanoes

INDEX